Make Me Laugh!

Ivan to Make You Laugh

JOKES AND NOVEL, NIFTY, AND NOTORIOUS NAMES

by Sam Schultz, with
Scott K. Peterson, and Rick and Ann Walton
pictures by Brian Gable

Carolrhoda Books, Inc. • Minneapolis

Q: Who used the first vacuum cleaner?
A: Colleen House.

Knock, Knock. Who's there?
Ivan. Ivan, who?
Ivan to come in!

Q: What do you call a boy who makes
your voice louder?
A: Mike.

Knock, Knock. Who's there?

Luke. Luke, who?

Luke, I'm standing on my head!

Q: Who invented glasses?

A: Otto Focus.

Q: Who makes the best dessert?

A: Angel Cake.

Knock, Knock. Who's there?

Annie. Annie, who?

Annie body home?

Q: Who has a wet face and an apple in his mouth?

A: Bob.

Knock, Knock. Who's there?

Ellis. Ellis, who?

Ellis the twelfth letter of the alphabet.

Q: Who ate the first hot dog?

A: Frank Furter.

Knock, Knock. Who's there?

Ben. Ben, who?

Ben looking all over for you.

Q: What girl has the sweetest personality?

A: Marsha Mellow.

Q: What man went broke buying oil?

A: Rusty Gate.

Knock, Knock. Who's there?

Abby. Abby, who?

Abby birthday to you.

Q: Who made exercise popular?

A: Jim Nasium.

Q: What girl is just purr-fect?

A: Kitty.

Knock, Knock. Who's there?

Rhett. Rhett, who?

Rhett-y or not, here I come!

Q: Who ran fifty miles without a drink of water?

A: Willie Makeit.

Q: Who likes to catch fish?

A: Annette.

Knock, Knock. Who's there?

Dewey. Dewey, who?

Dewey have to go to school today?

Q: Who can always be found in the saddle?

A: Rhoda Horse.

Q: Who always dresses in red and white at Christmastime?

A: Candy Cane.

Knock, Knock. Who's there?

Isabel. Isabel, who?

Isabel louder than a knock?

Q: Who quit gymnastics because of poor balance?

A: Eileen Wright.

Q: What bicycle racer rode ten miles but couldn't make it to the finish line?

A: Carrie Meback.

Knock, Knock. Who's there?

Shelby. Shelby, who?

Shelby comin' round the mountain when she comes!

Q: What girl likes to ride sailboats?

A: Wendy Day.

Q: Who falls off his raft into shallow water?

A: Wade.

Knock, Knock. Who's there?

Candy. Candy, who?

Candy-magine why you'd want to know.

Q: Who is a gas station's best customer?

A: Phil Mytank.

Q: Who comes to the gas station with Phil Mytank?

A: Aaron Mytires.

Knock, Knock. Who's there?

Boyd. Boyd, who?

Boydo you ask a lot of questions.

Q: Who always has a shovel in his hand?

A: Doug Pits.

Q: What do you get when you cross a cantaloupe with a guy named Walter?

A: A Waltermelon.

Q: Who has scratches all over his face from his mean cat?

A: Claude.

Knock, Knock. Who's there?

Emma. Emma, who?

Emma going to the store. Want to come along?

Q: Who likes to drive across the country?

A: Miles Togo.

Q: Who is the most fearless mountain climber?

A: Cliff Hanger.

Knock, Knock. Who's there?

Sam. Sam, who?

Sam times you make me so mad!

Q: What man delivers cargo from one state to another?

A: Mack Truck.

Q: Who taught ranchers to mark their cattle for identification?

A: Brandon Iron.

Q: What woman takes the blame for everything?

A: Paula Jize.

Knock, Knock. Who's there?

Daniel. Daniel, who?

Daniel so loud. I can hear you.

Q: Who got kicked out of school for goofing off?

A: Hank E. Pankie.

Knock, Knock. Who's there?

Vera. Vera, who?

Vera great team, aren't we?

Q: What man raises birds?

A: Barney Swallow.

Q: Who crossed the street without using the crosswalk?

A: Jay Walker.

Q: What man was arrested by mistake?
A: N. O. Cent.

Knock, Knock. Who's there?
Winnie. Winnie, who?
Winnie you gonna let me in?

Q: Who discovered the difference between reptiles and amphibians?
A: Sally Mander.

Knock, Knock. Who's there?
Lena. Lena, who?
Lena a little closer, and I'll whisper in your ear.

Q: What woman fenced in her whole farm?
A: Barb Wire.

Knock, Knock. Who's there?

Francis. Francis, who?

Francis where the Statue of Liberty comes from.

Q: Who was the first person to get paid for working?

A: Erna Living.

Q: Who is a good housekeeper?

A: Dustin.

Knock, Knock. Who's there?

Mabel. Mabel, who?

Mabel I'll tell you, and mabel I won't.

Q: What do you call a girl who babbles?
A: Brooke.

Q: What girl thinks frogs make the best pets?
A: Lilly Pads.

Knock, Knock. Who's there?
Juan. Juan, who?
Juan, two, three, four.

Q: Who is almost late for school every day?
A: Justin Time.

Q: What customer is welcome in any store?
A: Bill Paid.

Knock, Knock. Who's there?
Rita. Rita, who?
Rita book and you might learn something.

Q: Who made money selling strawberries?
A: Barry Picker.

Knock, Knock. Who's there?
Sawyer. Sawyer, who?
Sawyer lights on, so thought I'd stop by and say hello.

Q: Who can you always find in the sun?
A: Sandy Beach.

Knock, Knock. Who's there?
Doris. Doris, who?
Doris open, come on in.

Q: Who puts pretty designs on bowls?
A: Crystal Glass.

Knock, Knock. Who's there?
Henny. Henny, who?
Henny body wanna jump rope?

Q: What girl is allergic to cotton and wool?
A: Polly Esther.

Knock, Knock. Who's there?
Roxanne. Roxanne, who?
Roxanne stones may break my bones, but names can never hurt me.

Q: What do you call a girl who talks up a storm?

A: Gail.

Knock, Knock. Who's there?
Hugo. Hugo, who?
Hugo to the head of the class.

Q: Who hates dandelions?
A: Moe Grass.

Q: What man refuses to take hot baths?
A: Luke Warm.

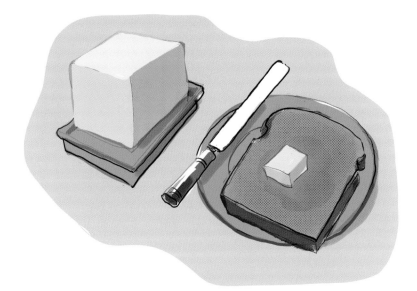

Q: Who never uses butter on her toast?

A: Marge Orin.

Q: Who tries to keep her hair out of her eyes?

A: Bobby Pin.

Knock, Knock. Who's there?

Otto. Otto, who?

Otto know if you don't.

Q: Who was always too nervous to sit down?

A: Stan Dup.

Q: Who has the most powerful weapons in space?

A: Ray Gun.

Knock, Knock. Who's there?

Harris. Harris, who?

Harris another name for a rabbit.

Q: Who always has a needle and thread?

A: Tara Shirt.

Q: Who locks herself out of the house at least once a day?

A: Dora Closed.

Knock, Knock. Who's there?

Olive. Olive, who?

Olive right down the street. Where do you live?

Q: Who can you put in your pocket?

A: Minnie.

Q: Who drinks up all the water in the bathtub?

A: Dwayne.

Knock, Knock. Who's there?

Paul. Paul, who?

Paul over, buddy, you're driving too fast.

Q: Who has trouble using a razor blade?

A: Harry Cheeks.

Knock, Knock. Who's there?

Kent. Kent, who?

Kent you see I'm too busy to talk to you?

Q: What do you call a boy who finds gold?

A: Rich.

Q: Who has only one cent to her name?

A: Penny.

Knock, Knock. Who's there?

Benny. Benny, who?

Benny for your thoughts.

Q: Who doesn't have five cents to his name?

A: Nicolas.

Q: Who was caught stealing cattle?

A: Russell Kows.

Knock, Knock. Who's there?

Carmen. Carmen, who?

Carmen over to my house!

Q: Who never pays back the money he borrows?

A: Owen.

Q: On what girl do people hang their coats?

A: Peg.

Knock, Knock. Who's there?

Cecil. Cecil, who?

Cecil have music wherever she goes.

Q: Who borrows money from banks and doesn't pay it back?

A: Robin.

Q: Who throws things?

A: Chuck.

Knock, Knock. Who's there?

Ron. Ron, who?

Ron and get me a glass of water.

Q: Who has to comb his arms?

A: Harry.

Knock, Knock. Who's there?

Dustin. Dustin, who?

Dustin' and makin' my bed are two things I don't like to do.

Knock, Knock. Who's there?

Russell. Russell, who?

Russell up some vittles, pardner. I'm starved!

Q: What do you call two people who are looking for a contact lens?

A: Hans and Denise.

Knock, Knock. Who's there?

Jess. Jess, who?

Jess you and me, kid.

Q: Who uses binoculars?

A: Seymour.

Q: What do you call a boy with big eyes?

A: Luke.

Knock, Knock. Who's there?

Tim. Tim, who?

Tim-ber!!

Q: What do you call a driver who doesn't look where he's going?

A: Rex.

Q: What do you call a cowboy with a hot iron?

A: Brandon.

Q: What do you call a boy who's always sunny?

A: Ray.

Knock, Knock. Who's there?

Fido. Fido, who?

Fidon't you call me on Saturday.

Q: Who leaves the ballpark because people keep hitting him?

A: Homer.

Q: Who always eats ketchup instead of mustard?

A: Tom Mato.

Knock, Knock. Who's there?
Everett. Everett, who?
Everett all the spinach on your plate?

Q: Who doesn't know where she's going?
A: Wanda.

Q: Who makes your skin turn brown?
A: Tanya.

Knock, Knock. Who's there?
Max. Max, who?
Max no difference to me!

Q: Who agrees with everything?
A: Kay.

Knock, Knock. Who's there?
Carson. Carson, who?
Carson the highway make lots of smog.

Q: What do you call a boy who's crackers?

A: Graham.

Knock, Knock. Who's there?

Wendy. Wendy, who?

Wendy you want to come out and play?

Q: Who goes a long way?

A: Miles.

Q: Who has a spring in her step?

A: May.

Knock, Knock. Who's there?

Justin. Justin, who?

Justin old friend here to see you.

Q: Who is covered in sugar glaze and bobs up and down in a cup of hot chocolate?

A: Duncan.

Knock, Knock. Who's there?

Rhoda. Rhoda, who?

Rhoda horse yesterday and fell off.

Q: Who's clumsy with knives?

A: Nick.

Q: Who has been out in the rain for too long?

A: Rusty.

Knock, Knock. Who's there?

Sarah. Sarah, who?

Sarah doorbell around here? I'm tired of knocking!

Q: Who do you send where you don't want to go?

A: Hugo.

Knock, Knock. Who's there?

Heidi. Heidi, who?

Heidi-n here, they'll never find us!

Q: Who do people step on before they go into the house?

A: Matt.

Q: Who lifts cars?

A: Jack.

Q: What do you call a boy who bothers you like a pesky insect?

A: Nat.

Knock, Knock. Who's there?

Maya. Maya, who?

Maya have a nice pair of shoes!

Q: Who falls into the fireplace and goes up the chimney?

A: Ashley.

Q: Who lies across rivers and lets cars drive over her?

A: Bridget.

This book is available in two editions:
Library binding by Carolrhoda Books, Inc.,
    a division of Lerner Publishing Group
Soft cover by First Avenue Editions,
    an imprint of Lerner Publishing Group
241 First Avenue North
Minneapolis, MN 55401 U.S.A.

Website address: www.carolrhodabooks.com

Library of Congress Cataloging-in-Publication Data

Schultz, Sam.
    Ivan to make you laugh : jokes and novel, nifty, and notorious names / by Sam
Schultz ... [et al.] ; pictures by Brian Gable.
        p.   cm. — (Make me laugh!)
    Summary: Presents a variety of jokes about people's names.
    ISBN: 1–57505–659–3 (lib. bdg. : alk. paper)
    ISBN: 1–57505–734–4 (pbk. : alk. paper)
    1. Names, Personal—Juvenile humor. 2. Wit and humor, Juvenile. [1. Names,
Personal—Humor. 2. Jokes.] I. Schultz, Sam. II. Gable, Brian, 1949– ill.
III. Series.
PN6231.N24I93 2005
818'.60208—dc22   2003019243

Manufactured in the United States of America
1 2 3 4 5 6 – DP – 10 09 08 07 06 05